Pebble Plus

Living in a Biome

Life in a Polar Region

by Carol K. Lindeen

Consulting Editor: Gail Saunders-Smith, Ph.D.

Consultant: Sandra Mather, Professor Emerita
Department of Geology and Astronomy, West Chester University
West Chester, Pennsylvania

Capstone
press

Mankato, Minnesota

Pebble Plus is published by Capstone Press
151 Good Counsel Drive, P.O. Box 669, Mankato, Minnesota 56002
http://www.capstone-press.com

1 2 3 4 5 6 08 07 06 05 04 03

Library of Congress Cataloging-in-Publication Data
Lindeen, Carol K., 1976–
    Life in a polar region / by Carol K. Lindeen.
    p. cm.—(Pebble plus: Living in a biome)
    Includes bibliographical references (p. 23) and index.
    Summary: Simple text and photographs introduce the polar region biome,
including the environment, plants, and animals.
    ISBN 0-7368-2100-7 (hardcover)
    1. Natural history—Polar regions—Juvenile literature. [1. Natural history—Polar regions.]
I. Title.
QH84.1 .L56 2004
578'.0911—dc21   2002155689

Editorial Credits
Martha E. H. Rustad, editor; Kia Adams, designer and illustrator; Juliette Peters, cover production designer; Kelly Garvin, photo researcher;
   Eric Kudalis, product planning editor

Photo Credits
Corbis, cover, 14–15
Digital Vision, 1, 6–7, 8–9, 12–13
Houserstock/Dave G. Houser, 4–5
Minden Pictures/Jim Brandenburg, 16–17
Tom Stack & Associates/Thomas Kitchin, 10–11; Erwin & Peggy Bauer, 20–21
Visuals Unlimited/Gerald & Buff Corsi, 18–19

Note to Parents and Teachers

The Living in a Biome series supports national science standards related to life science. This book describes and illustrates animal and plant life in polar regions. The photographs support early readers in understanding the text. This book also introduces early readers to subject-specific vocabulary words, which are defined in the Glossary section. Early readers may need assistance to read some words and to use the Table of Contents, Glossary, Read More, Internet Sites, and Index/Word List sections of the book.

Word Count: 133
Early-Intervention Level: 13

Table of Contents

What Are Polar Regions?

A polar region is a very cold place. Ice, snow, and water cover polar regions.

Polar regions are found
near the North Pole and
the South Pole.

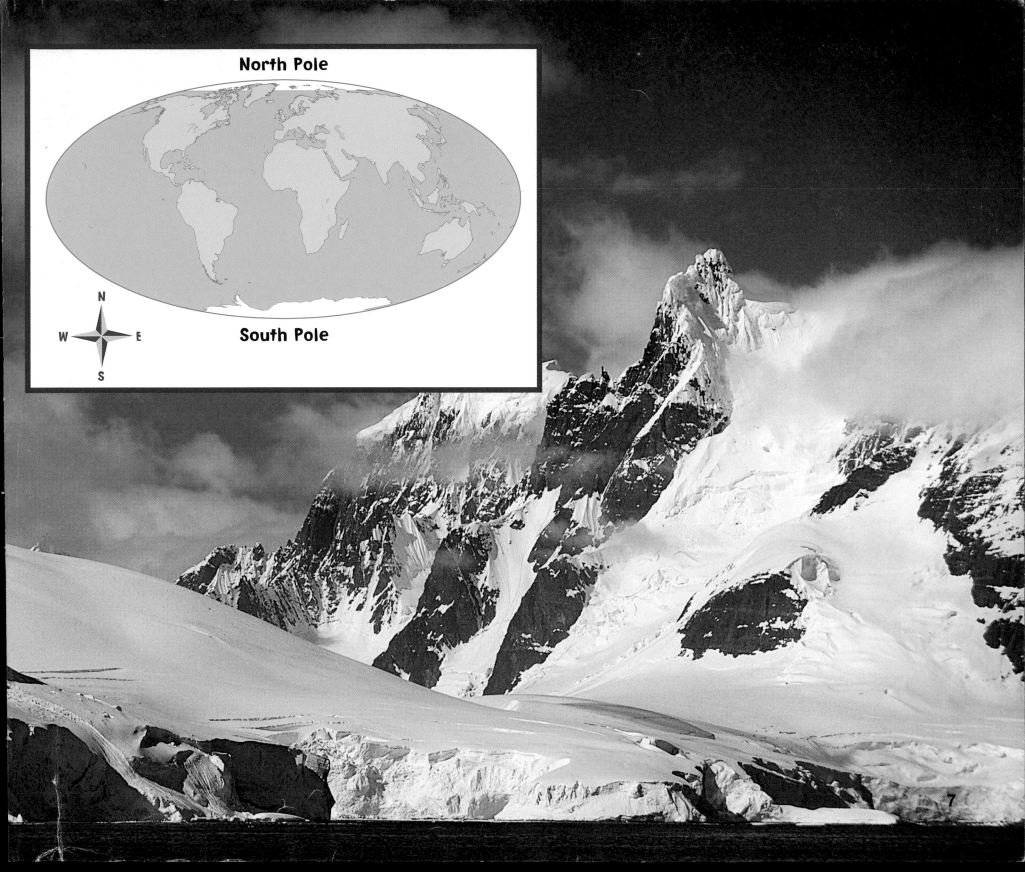

North Pole

South Pole

W N E S

Polar Animals

Polar bears have thick, warm fur. Polar bears swim and catch fish.

Seals can be gray, white, or
brown. Seals have flippers
that help them swim.

Penguins dive into the ocean to look for food. Penguins catch fish with their strong beaks.

Arctic foxes curl up
in their long, bushy tails
to stay warm.

Polar Plants

Few plants live in polar regions. The cold, windy weather makes it hard for plants to grow.

Moss and other small
plants grow on rocks
and near water.

Living Together

White snow hides some polar animals as they hunt for food. Melting snow gives water to polar plants. Polar regions are full of life.

Glossary

beak—the hard part of a bird's mouth

flipper—a flat limb with bones; sea animals can walk and swim using their flippers.

moss—a soft, short plant with no roots; moss grows on damp soil, rocks, and tree trunks.

North Pole—the most northern point on Earth; the area around the North Pole is called the Arctic; the Arctic is covered with ice and snow.

penguin—a black and white bird with short legs; penguins cannot fly, but they can swim; some penguins live at the South Pole.

region—a large area

South Pole—the most southern point on Earth; the area around the South Pole is called the Antarctic; the Antarctic is covered with ice and snow.

Read More

Gray, Susan H. *Tundra.* First Reports. Minneapolis: Compass Point Books, 2001.

Murphy, Patricia J. *Why Are the North and South Poles So Cold?* The Library of Why? New York: PowerKids Press, 2003.

Snedden, Robert. *Around the Poles.* Habitats. North Mankato, Minn.: Smart Apple Media, 2003.

Internet Sites

Do you want to find out more about polar regions?
Let FactHound, our fact-finding hound dog, do the research for you.

Here's how:

1) Visit *http://www.facthound.com*

2) Type in the **Book ID** number: **0736821007**

3) Click on **FETCH IT**.

FactHound will fetch Internet sites picked by our editors just for you!

Index/Word List